# DR. ERIC JOHNSON

# THE COLOR OF MY JOY

## A PERSONAL DEVELOPMENT WORKBOOK

### ILLUSTRATED BY: GLENN BREWER

CITI OF BOOKS

Copyright © 2025 by Eric L. Johnson, PhD

All rights reserved. No part of this publication may be reproduced, distributed, or transmitted in any form or by any means, including, photocopying,recording, or other electronic or mechanical methods, without the prior written permission of the copyright owner and the publisher, except in the case of brief quotations embodied in critical reviews and certain other noncommercial uses permitted by copyright law. For permission requests, write to the publisher, addressed "Attention: Permissions Coordinator," at the address below.

**CITIOFBOOKS, INC.**
3736 Eubank NE Suite A1
Albuquerque, NM 87111-3579
*www.citiofbooks.com*
Hotline:       1 (877) 389-2759
Fax:            1 (505) 930-7244

Ordering Information:
Quantity sales. Special discounts are available on quantity purchases by corporations, associations, and others. For details, contact the publisher at the address above.

Printed in the United States of America.
ISBN-13:     Paperback       979-8-90124-136-3
                    eBook              979-8-90124-137-0

## Introduction: Color, Joy, Wellness and Me

**Color and Joy**

Joy is a positive emotion often linked to bright, vibrant colors. Colors like yellow, orange, and pink are typically associated with feelings of joy, playfulness, and warmth. This connection is evident in celebrations, where decorations and clothing are chosen specifically to create a joyous mood.

On a psychological level, exposure to certain colors can increase serotonin levels, which are associated with feelings of well-being and happiness. This is why spending time in colorful environments, such as gardens or art installations, can uplift our mood and enhance our sense of joy.

While there are universal trends in color-emotion associations, cultural background, and personal experiences also shape how individuals respond to colors. For example, white is associated with purity and weddings in some cultures, but with mourning in others. Personal memories and preferences further influence these emotional connections.

This activity book seeks to invite users to invest in their own wellness and joy by exploring how color feeds your spirit and how that impression affects the visual interpretation of the world you perceive. Color is in some ways incredibly surface and in others significantly relevant. The role color can play in the various ways we interact with our environment can be significant. In this book you will choose colors to explore intimate and deeply personal connections to your thoughts and feelings. Colors can promote calmness or creativity. Moreover, Art and therapy can help us all regulate, understand, and process our emotions and experiences.

## Conclusion

This book offers color as more than a visual experience, we invite those who wish to take the journey, to consider color as a powerful tool for communicating and evoking emotion. Understanding the relationship between color and our feelings can help us make choices that enhance our joy and emotional well-being. By embracing the emotional impact of color, we can create more vibrant, positive, and expressive lives. It is the deepest hope of the author that all who utilize this tool, find a pathway to wellness and joy that is both challenging and fulfilling. The journey is yours, make of it what you will.

## Illustrator's Information

Glenn Brewer is an award-winning illustrator and comic creator. He has BFA in Fine Arts from the Columbus College of Art and Design, where he received training in graphic design, color theory, perspective drawing, and both traditional and digital media.

His illustration clients include: TSR Inc, Wizards of the Coast, Visionary Entertainment Studios, New Orleans Tribune, Frost Illustrated, Tygeron Graphics, Graphic Classics, Mythworlde Media, Webway Comics, 2nd Look Oncology Consultants, and Unchained Spirit Enterprises, a children's book publisher.

*Guidance on your journey:*

There are no recipes or instructions, the journey is yours and yours alone. Each image in this process is an invitation to explore, discover and share space with a version of joy that speaks to your spirit.

**Suggested sequence.**

1.) Before engaging each image close your eyes and take 3 deep breaths.

2.) Color each image any color of your choosing, take note of why you chose the color and be aware of what you think the color invites you to feel.

3.) Reflect on the process; what you thought or felt? Be intentional about the notion of Joy and what about it challenges you.

"TAKE CARE OF THE PEOPLE YOU LOVE
BUT TAKE EVEN BETTER CARE OF THE PEOPLE WHO LOVE YOU."

What does the image invite you to think about or consider?

_____
_____
_____
_____
_____
_____
_____
_____
_____
_____
_____
_____
_____
_____
_____

What colors come to mind and why?

_____
_____
_____
_____
_____
_____
_____
_____
_____
_____
_____
_____
_____
_____
_____

✣ Color the image ✣

How did the colors speak to your spirit?

___

What are you noticing about yourself and what you are learning about your understanding of your perception of joy?

Additional notes (anything you wish to note to yourself?)

"IF YOU LIVE YOUR LIFE IN FEAR
YOU INVITE THE PRESENCE OF ALL THE THINGS THAT SCARE YOU."

What does the image invite you to think about or consider?

_____

What colors come to mind and why?

_____

✷✷ Color the image ✷✷

How did the colors speak to your spirit?

_____
_____
_____
_____
_____
_____
_____
_____
_____
_____
_____
_____
_____

What are you noticing about yourself and what you are learning about your understanding of your perception of joy?

_____
_____
_____
_____
_____
_____
_____
_____
_____
_____
_____
_____
_____
_____

Additional notes (anything you wish to note to yourself?)

"BELIEF ISN'T ABOUT WHAT YOU CAN SEE, IT'S ABOUT WHAT YOU CAN'T."

What does the image invite you to think about or consider?

_____
_____
_____
_____
_____
_____
_____
_____
_____
_____
_____
_____

What colors come to mind and why?

_____
_____
_____
_____
_____
_____
_____
_____
_____
_____
_____
_____
_____

✺ Color the image ✺

How did the colors speak to your spirit?

_____
_____
_____
_____
_____
_____
_____
_____
_____
_____
_____
_____

What are you noticing about yourself and what you are learning about your understanding of your perception of joy?

_____
_____
_____
_____
_____
_____
_____
_____
_____
_____
_____
_____
_____
_____

Additional notes (anything you wish to note to yourself?)

"BEFORE YOU FEED IT TO YOUR SOUL
BE SURE YOU STUDY THE INGREDIENTS"

What does the image invite you to think about or consider?

_____
_____
_____
_____
_____
_____
_____
_____
_____
_____
_____
_____
_____
_____
_____

What colors come to mind and why?

_____
_____
_____
_____
_____
_____
_____
_____
_____
_____
_____
_____
_____
_____
_____

✳✳ Color the image ✳✳

How did the colors speak to your spirit?

_____
_____
_____
_____
_____
_____
_____
_____
_____
_____
_____
_____
_____

What are you noticing about yourself and what you are learning about your understanding of your perception of joy?

_____
_____
_____
_____
_____
_____
_____
_____
_____
_____
_____
_____
_____
_____

Additional notes (anything you wish to note to yourself?)

What am I learning about myself that I haven't noticed before? Are there things about me that I understand differently? Things I need to remind myself about me.

___

What am I doing that I need to stop doing for my own growth, development, and joy?

___

What am I not doing that I need to start doing to own my growth, development, and Joy?

_____
_____
_____
_____
_____
_____
_____
_____
_____
_____
_____
_____

What in this process matters to me right now?

_____
_____
_____
_____
_____
_____
_____
_____
_____
_____
_____
_____

"IN THIS WORLD YOU CAN BE ANYTHING YOU WANT JUST DON'T BE UNGRATEFUL."

What does the image invite you to think about or consider?

_____

What colors come to mind and why?

_____

✳︎ Color the image ✳︎

How did the colors speak to your spirit?

_____
_____
_____
_____
_____
_____
_____
_____
_____
_____
_____
_____
_____

What are you noticing about yourself and what you are learning about your understanding of your perception of joy?

_____
_____
_____
_____
_____
_____
_____
_____
_____
_____
_____
_____
_____

Additional notes (anything you wish to note to yourself?)
_____
_____
_____
_____
_____
_____
_____
_____
_____
_____
_____
_____
_____
_____
_____
_____
_____
_____
_____
_____

What does the image invite you to think about or consider?

_____
_____
_____
_____
_____
_____
_____
_____
_____
_____
_____
_____

What colors come to mind and why?

_____
_____
_____
_____
_____
_____
_____
_____
_____
_____
_____
_____
_____

✺ Color the image ✺

How did the colors speak to your spirit?

_____
_____
_____
_____
_____
_____
_____
_____
_____
_____
_____
_____

What are you noticing about yourself and what you are learning about your understanding of your perception of joy?

_____
_____
_____
_____
_____
_____
_____
_____
_____
_____
_____
_____

Additional notes (anything you wish to note to yourself?)

"WE DONT INHERIT THE WORLD FROM OUR PARENTS,
WE BORROW IT FROM OUR CHILDREN."

What does the image invite you to think about or consider?

_____
_____
_____
_____
_____
_____
_____
_____
_____
_____
_____
_____

What colors come to mind and why?

_____
_____
_____
_____
_____
_____
_____
_____
_____
_____
_____
_____

✲✲ Color the image ✲✲

How did the colors speak to your spirit?

_____
_____
_____
_____
_____
_____
_____
_____
_____
_____
_____

What are you noticing about yourself and what you are learning about your understanding of your perception of joy?

_____
_____
_____
_____
_____
_____
_____
_____
_____
_____
_____

Additional notes (anything you wish to note to yourself)?

_____
_____
_____
_____
_____
_____
_____
_____
_____
_____
_____
_____
_____
_____
_____
_____
_____
_____
_____
_____

"WE OFTEN TAKE FOR GRANTED THE VERY THINGS THAT DESERVE OUR GRATITUDE."

What does the image invite you to think about or consider?

_____
_____
_____
_____
_____
_____
_____
_____
_____
_____
_____
_____

What colors come to mind and why?

_____
_____
_____
_____
_____
_____
_____
_____
_____
_____
_____
_____
_____

✱✱ Color the image ✱✱

How did the colors speak to your spirit?

_____
_____
_____
_____
_____
_____
_____
_____
_____
_____
_____

What are you noticing about yourself and what you are learning about your understanding of your perception of joy?

_____
_____
_____
_____
_____
_____
_____
_____
_____
_____
_____
_____

Additional notes (anything you wish to note to yourself?)

_____
_____
_____
_____
_____
_____
_____
_____
_____
_____
_____
_____
_____
_____
_____
_____
_____
_____
_____
_____

What am I learning about myself that I haven't noticed before? Are there things about me that I understand differently? Things I need to remind myself about me.

_____
_____
_____
_____
_____
_____
_____
_____
_____
_____

What am I doing that I need to stop doing for my own growth, development, and joy?

_____
_____
_____
_____
_____
_____
_____
_____
_____
_____

What am I not doing that I need to start doing to own my growth, development, and Joy?

_____
_____
_____
_____
_____
_____
_____
_____
_____
_____
_____

What in this process matters to me right now?

_____
_____
_____
_____
_____
_____
_____
_____
_____
_____
_____
_____

"I HAVE LEARNED THAT YOU CAN KEEP GOING LONG AFTER YOU THINK YOU CAN'T."

What does the image invite you to think about or consider?

_____
_____
_____
_____
_____
_____
_____
_____
_____
_____
_____
_____
_____
_____

What colors come to mind and why?

_____
_____
_____
_____
_____
_____
_____
_____
_____
_____
_____
_____
_____
_____

✷✷ Color the image ✷✷

How did the colors speak to your spirit?

_____
_____
_____
_____
_____
_____
_____
_____
_____
_____
_____
_____

What are you noticing about yourself and what you are learning about your understanding of your perception of joy?

_____
_____
_____
_____
_____
_____
_____
_____
_____
_____
_____
_____
_____

Additional notes (anything you wish to note to yourself?)

_____
_____
_____
_____
_____
_____
_____
_____
_____
_____
_____
_____
_____
_____
_____
_____
_____
_____
_____
_____

"THERE IS NO SOUND, NO VOICE, NO CRY IN ALL THE WORLD THAT CAN BE HEARD UNTIL SOMEONE LISTENS."

What does the image invite you to think about or consider?

_____
_____
_____
_____
_____
_____
_____
_____
_____
_____
_____
_____
_____

What colors come to mind and why?

_____
_____
_____
_____
_____
_____
_____
_____
_____
_____
_____
_____
_____

✳✳ Color the image ✳✳

How did the colors speak to your spirit?

_____
_____
_____
_____
_____
_____
_____
_____
_____
_____
_____
_____

What are you noticing about yourself and what you are learning about your understanding of your perception of joy?

_____
_____
_____
_____
_____
_____
_____
_____
_____
_____
_____
_____
_____

Additional notes (anything you wish to note to yourself?)

WE ARE BLESSED IF WE SHARE SPACE
WITH PEOPLE WHO CARE AS MUCH FOR OUR SPIRIT AS THEY DO FOR OUR BODIES.

What does the image invite you to think about or consider?

_____
_____
_____
_____
_____
_____
_____
_____
_____
_____
_____
_____
_____

What colors come to mind and why?

_____
_____
_____
_____
_____
_____
_____
_____
_____
_____
_____
_____
_____
_____

✸✸ Color the image ✸✸

How did the colors speak to your spirit?

_____
_____
_____
_____
_____
_____
_____
_____
_____
_____
_____
_____
_____

What are you noticing about yourself and what you are learning about your understanding of your perception of joy?

_____
_____
_____
_____
_____
_____
_____
_____
_____
_____
_____
_____
_____

Additional notes (anything you wish to note to yourself?)
___

"MISTAKES ARE PROOF THAT YOU ARE TRYING!"

What does the image invite you to think about or consider?

_____
_____
_____
_____
_____
_____
_____
_____
_____
_____
_____
_____

What colors come to mind and why?

_____
_____
_____
_____
_____
_____
_____
_____
_____
_____
_____
_____

✼✼ Color the image ✼✼

How did the colors speak to your spirit?

_____

What are you noticing about yourself and what you are learning about your understanding of your perception of joy?

_____

Addition notes (anything you wish to note to yourself?)

What am I learning about myself that I haven't noticed before? Are there things about me that I understand differently? Things I need to remind myself about me.

_____
_____
_____
_____
_____
_____
_____
_____
_____
_____
_____
_____

What am I doing that I need to stop doing for my own growth, development, and joy?

_____
_____
_____
_____
_____
_____
_____
_____
_____
_____
_____
_____

What am I not doing that I need to start doing to own my growth, development, and Joy?

_____
_____
_____
_____
_____
_____
_____
_____
_____
_____
_____
_____
_____

What in this process matters to me right now?

_____
_____
_____
_____
_____
_____
_____
_____
_____
_____
_____
_____
_____
_____

"CONSIDER AND ACT UPON SOMETHING GREATER THAN YOURSELF TODAY."

What does the image invite you to think about or consider?

_____
_____
_____
_____
_____
_____
_____
_____
_____
_____
_____
_____
_____

What colors come to mind and why?

_____
_____
_____
_____
_____
_____
_____
_____
_____
_____
_____
_____
_____

✲✲ Color the image ✲✲

How did the colors speak to your spirit?

___

What are you noticing about yourself and what you are learning about your understanding of your perception of joy?

___

Additional notes (anything you wish to note to yourself?)

"YOU DON'T LOSE TRUE FRIENDS IN THE DARK,
THEY GRAB YOUR HAND AND HELP GUIDE YOU TOWARD THE LIGHT."

What does the image invite you to think about or consider?

_____
_____
_____
_____
_____
_____
_____
_____
_____
_____
_____
_____
_____
_____

What colors come to mind and why?

_____
_____
_____
_____
_____
_____
_____
_____
_____
_____
_____
_____
_____

⁂ Color the image ⁂

How did the colors speak to your spirit?

_____
_____
_____
_____
_____
_____
_____
_____
_____
_____
_____
_____
_____

What are you noticing about yourself and what you are learning about your understanding of your perception of joy?

_____
_____
_____
_____
_____
_____
_____
_____
_____
_____
_____
_____
_____
_____

Additional notes (anything you wish to note to yourself?)

_____
_____
_____
_____
_____
_____
_____
_____
_____
_____
_____
_____
_____
_____
_____
_____
_____
_____
_____
_____

"EVERYTHING IN THIS LIFE WORTH HAVING IS BETTER WHEN IT IS SHARED."

What does the image invite you to think about or consider?

_____
_____
_____
_____
_____
_____
_____
_____
_____
_____
_____
_____
_____

What colors come to mind and why?

_____
_____
_____
_____
_____
_____
_____
_____
_____
_____
_____
_____
_____
_____

⁂ Color the image ⁂

How did the colors speak to your spirit?

_____
_____
_____
_____
_____
_____
_____
_____
_____
_____
_____
_____

What are you noticing about yourself and what you are learning about your understanding of your perception of joy?

_____
_____
_____
_____
_____
_____
_____
_____
_____
_____
_____
_____
_____

Additional notes (anything you wish to note to yourself?)
_____
_____
_____
_____
_____
_____
_____
_____
_____
_____
_____
_____
_____
_____
_____
_____
_____
_____

"DEATH IS NOT OUR GREATEST LOSS, OUR GREATEST LOSS IS THAT WHICH DIES WITHIN US WHILE WE YET LIVE. LIVE YA BEST LIFE WHILE YOU GOT IT."

What does the image invite you to think about or consider?

_____
_____
_____
_____
_____
_____
_____
_____
_____
_____
_____
_____
_____

What colors come to mind and why?

_____
_____
_____
_____
_____
_____
_____
_____
_____
_____
_____
_____
_____

✣ Color the image ✣

How did the colors speak to your spirit?

_____
_____
_____
_____
_____
_____
_____
_____
_____
_____
_____
_____

What are you noticing about yourself and what you are learning about your understanding of your perception of joy?

_____
_____
_____
_____
_____
_____
_____
_____
_____
_____
_____
_____
_____

Additional notes (anything you wish to note to yourself?)
_____
_____
_____
_____
_____
_____
_____
_____
_____
_____
_____
_____
_____
_____
_____
_____
_____
_____
_____
_____

What am I learning about myself that I haven't noticed before? Are there things about me that I understand differently? Things I need to remind myself about me.

_____
_____
_____
_____
_____
_____
_____
_____
_____
_____
_____
_____

What am I doing that I need to stop doing for my own growth, development, and joy?

_____
_____
_____
_____
_____
_____
_____
_____
_____
_____
_____
_____

What am I not doing that I need to start doing to own my growth, development, and Joy?

_____
_____
_____
_____
_____
_____
_____
_____
_____
_____
_____

What in this process matters to me right now?

_____
_____
_____
_____
_____
_____
_____
_____
_____
_____
_____
_____

What does the image invite you to think about or consider?

_____
_____
_____
_____
_____
_____
_____
_____
_____
_____
_____
_____
_____

What colors come to mind and why?

_____
_____
_____
_____
_____
_____
_____
_____
_____
_____
_____
_____
_____

✨ Color the image ✨

How did the colors speak to your spirit?

_____
_____
_____
_____
_____
_____
_____
_____
_____
_____
_____
_____

What are you noticing about yourself and what you are learning about your understanding of your perception of joy?

_____
_____
_____
_____
_____
_____
_____
_____
_____
_____
_____
_____
_____

Additional notes (anything you wish to note to yourself?)

_____
_____
_____
_____
_____
_____
_____
_____
_____
_____
_____
_____
_____
_____
_____
_____
_____
_____
_____
_____

What does the image invite you to think about or consider?

_____
_____
_____
_____
_____
_____
_____
_____
_____
_____
_____
_____

What colors come to mind and why?

_____
_____
_____
_____
_____
_____
_____
_____
_____
_____
_____
_____

⁎⁎ Color the image ⁎⁎

How did the colors speak to your spirit?

_____
_____
_____
_____
_____
_____
_____
_____
_____
_____
_____
_____

What are you noticing about yourself and what you are learning about your understanding of your perception of joy?

_____
_____
_____
_____
_____
_____
_____
_____
_____
_____
_____
_____

Additional notes (anything you wish to note to yourself?)

_____
_____
_____
_____
_____
_____
_____
_____
_____
_____
_____
_____
_____
_____
_____
_____
_____
_____
_____
_____
_____

What does the image invite you to think about or consider?

_____
_____
_____
_____
_____
_____
_____
_____
_____
_____
_____
_____

What colors come to mind and why?

_____
_____
_____
_____
_____
_____
_____
_____
_____
_____
_____
_____

✱✱ Color the image ✱✱

How did the colors speak to your spirit?

_____
_____
_____
_____
_____
_____
_____
_____
_____
_____
_____

What are you noticing about yourself and what you are learning about your understanding of your perception of joy?

_____
_____
_____
_____
_____
_____
_____
_____
_____
_____
_____
_____
_____

Additional notes (anything you wish to note to yourself?)

What am I learning about myself that I haven't noticed before? Are there things about me that I understand differently? Things I need to remind myself about me.

_____
_____
_____
_____
_____
_____
_____
_____
_____
_____
_____

What am I doing that I need to stop doing for my own growth, development, and joy?

_____
_____
_____
_____
_____
_____
_____
_____
_____
_____
_____

What am I not doing that I need to start doing to own my growth, development, and Joy?

_____
_____
_____
_____
_____
_____
_____
_____
_____
_____
_____
_____

What in this process matters to me right now?

_____
_____
_____
_____
_____
_____
_____
_____
_____
_____
_____
_____

The journey to understanding and sharing space with a version of joy that feeds your spirit is never an accident. It is always the result of the work we do to be better versions of ourselves as often as possible. It is an ongoing process that without question has ebbs and flows that require us to investigate who and what matters to us and why. The workbook is designed to be a tool for anyone who wishes to explore who they are from the inside out. Joy is a fundamental human emotion that can transform our daily experiences and overall outlook on life. Understanding what brings us joy is crucial, as it allows us to make intentional choices that promote happiness, resilience, and meaningful living.

Recognizing the sources of our joy is an act of self-awareness and survival. By giving our attention to moments that spark happiness and enhance our capacity to better understand what is in our interest—whether it's spending time with loved ones, pursuing hobbies, or achieving personal goals—we gain insight into our values and priorities. This awareness enables us to structure our lives in ways that align with what truly matters to us.

Life is filled with ups and downs. Knowing what brings us joy provides us with tools to cope during difficult times. Joyful activities and memories can serve as anchors, reminding us of the good in life and helping us recover from setbacks more quickly.

In summary, understanding what brings us joy is a cornerstone of a fulfilling, intentional, and resilient life. It empowers us to cultivate happiness, build meaningful relationships, and maintain mental well-being. By taking time to reflect on and pursue the things that make us joyful, we enrich our lives and the lives of those around us.

As I continue, notes to guide me on my journey……

www.ingramcontent.com/pod-product-compliance
Lightning Source LLC
Chambersburg PA
CBHW052033030426
42337CB00027B/4989